Pebble® Plus

Understanding Differences

Some Kids Are Blind

Revised Edition

by Lola M. Schaefer

CAPSTONE PRESS
a capstone imprint

Pebble Plus is published by Capstone Press,
1710 Roe Crest Drive, North Mankato, Minnesota 56003
www.mycapstone.com

Copyright © 2018 by Capstone Press, a Capstone imprint.
All rights reserved. No part of this publication may be reproduced in whole or in part, or stored in a retrieval system, or transmitted in any form or by any means, electronic, mechanical, photocopying, recording, or otherwise, without written permission of the publisher.

Library of Congress Cataloging-in-Publication Data is available on the Library of Congress website.
ISBN 978-1-5435-0996-0 (library binding)
ISBN 978-1-5435-1000-3 (paperback)
ISBN 978-1-5435-1004-1 (ebook pdf)

Editorial Credits
Sarah Bennett, designer; Tracy Cummins, media researcher; Tori Abraham, production specialist

Photo Credits
Capstone Studio: Karon Dubke, 5, 9; Getty Images: BLOOM image, 19, Majdi Fathi/NurPhoto, 21, mapodile, 7, Richard Hutchings, 17; Science Source: Amélie Benoist Khakurel, 13, Lawrence Migdale, Cover; Shutterstock: DoozyDo, Design Element, wavebreakmedia, 11; SuperStock: Spencer Grant/age fotostock, 15

Note to Parents and Teachers

The Understanding Differences set supports national social studies standards related to individual development and identity. This book describes and illustrates children who are blind. The images support early readers in understanding the text. The repetition of words and phrases helps early readers learn new words. This book also introduces early readers to subject-specific vocabulary words, which are defined in the Glossary section. Early readers may need assistance to read some words and to use the Table of Contents, Glossary, Read More, Internet Sites, Critical Thinking Questions, and Index sections of the book.

Printed in the United States 5678

Table of Contents

Blindness 4
Braille 10
Everyday Life 14
Glossary 22
Read More 23
Internet Sites 23
Critical Thinking Questions 24
Index 24

Blindness

Some kids are blind.

Kids who are blind

cannot see.

Some kids are blind
when they are born.
Some kids become
blind from a sickness
or from getting hurt.

Kids who are blind use their other senses. They hear their friends talking on the phone. They feel things around them.

MW112
MEDIA CENTER

Braille

Some kids who are blind read Braille. Braille is raised dots that stand for letters and numbers.

Some kids who are blind use Braille computers to do homework and send email.

Everyday Life

Some kids who are blind use white canes to guide them.

ESTD 2004

Adults who are blind
can use guide dogs.

Some kids who are blind enjoy listening to audiobooks.

Some kids who are blind

like to do karate.

Glossary

audiobook—a recording of someone reading a book aloud

blind—unable to see or having very limited sight; some people who are blind can see light and color

Braille—a set of raised dots that stand for letters and numbers; people use their fingertips to read the raised dots; Louis Braille of France invented Braille in the early 1800s

guide dog—a dog that is specially trained to lead adults who are blind; guide dogs help adults who are blind move safely in public places

senses—ways of learning about your surroundings; hearing, smelling, touching, tasting, and seeing are the five senses

Read More

Burcaw, Shane. *Not So Different.* New York: Roaring Brook Press, 2017.

Pettiford, Rebecca. *Different Abilities.* Celebrating Differences. Minneapolis: Jump!, Inc., 2017.

Internet Sites

Use FactHound to find Internet sites related to this book.

Visit *www.facthound.com*

Just type **9781543509960** and go.

Critical Thinking Questions

1. What is Braille? How does it help people who are blind?

2. How does a person who is blind use his or her other senses?

3. How would using a cane be helpful to a person who is blind?

Index

audiobooks, 18
Braille, 10, 12
computers, 12
email, 12
feel, 8
friends, 8
guide dogs, 16
hear, 8
homework, 12
karate, 20
listen, 18
phone, 8
senses, 8
sickness, 6
white canes, 14